HowI

How to Raise Miniature Horses

Your Step By Step Guide to Raising Miniature Horses

HowExpert with Christina Reilly

For more tips related to this topic, visit HowExpert.com/miniaturehorse.

Recommended Resources

- HowExpert.com – Quick 'How To' Guides on All Topics from A to Z by Everyday Experts.
- HowExpert.com/free – Free HowExpert Email Newsletter.
- HowExpert.com/books – HowExpert Books
- HowExpert.com/courses – HowExpert Courses
- HowExpert.com/clothing – HowExpert Clothing
- HowExpert.com/membership – HowExpert Membership Site
- HowExpert.com/affiliates – HowExpert Affiliate Program
- HowExpert.com/writers – Write About Your #1 Passion/Knowledge/Expertise & Become a HowExpert Author.
- HowExpert.com/resources – Additional HowExpert Recommended Resources
- YouTube.com/HowExpert – Subscribe to HowExpert YouTube.
- Instagram.com/HowExpert – Follow HowExpert on Instagram.
- Facebook.com/HowExpert – Follow HowExpert on Facebook

COPYRIGHT, LEGAL NOTICE AND DISCLAIMER:

Table of Contents

CHAPTER 1: THE HISTORY OF THE MINIATURE HORSE

Miniature horses have been around for a very long time. The history on them is actually quite interesting. French King Louis XIV (The Sun King) was known to keep a zoo full of unusual animals, which included miniature horses. This was at the Palace at Versailles in 1650 A.D. This is the earliest history found on these unique mini horses.

In the 1700s you could find miniature horses residing at noblemen's castles. They were bought for the children of aristocrats and the rich, for pets. By 1765 many paintings and articles featured the miniature horses. For a long time throughout history, horses have appeared in stories around the world and sometimes as magical creatures. From cave paintings to nursery rhymes, horses play a prominent part in art and literature all over.

However, not all miniature horses were pets of the kings and queens to be pampered. Some were used for work purposes or coal mine horses in the English Midlands, Wales and Northern Europe. They were referred to as pit ponies. Horses have been featured throughout our history, mainly as transport for knights and soldiers but also especially during times of war. These horses have been used for that with carriages, as well.

Miniature horses are found in many countries, particularly the Americas and Europe. The first miniature horses to be seen in the United States were in 1888, although they had been around a long time before that. Research shows that there was little public awareness of them until 1960.

The belief is that miniature horses utilized the blood of the English and the Dutch mine horses brought into this country in the 19th century. They were used in some Appalachian coal mines as late as 1950. They also have the blood of the Shetland pony, as well. Several of which appear in the bloodlines of some of the miniatures today.

The miniature horse is the result of nearly 400 years of selective breeding. Small horses were always present in the courts of Europe, where they were a popular pet for people to see. They also played a role in traveling circuses, where they gained a reputation for being enthusiastic performers.

In the last past few decades the miniature horses have been imported from many countries including England, West Germany, Belgium and Holland, while others have been selectively breeding down larger breeds of horses, in search of the perfect mini.

Throughout the miniature horse's past, the breed has been bred for many reasons. They were bred for research, novelty, pets, monetary gain, mining work, exhibition and also royal gifts.

At the turn of the 20th century many distinct smaller horse breeds came about. These breeds are what made up the horse breeds and then miniature horses were brought into the picture, in the United States of

America. They were the smallest horse breed possible. They were also a sized down breed of the full-sized horse breed.

There are two registries in the United States for this miniature horse breed, the American Miniature Horse Association (AMHA) and the American Miniature Horse Registry (AMHR). The AMHA was founded in July of 1978 and was interested in dedicating their time to establishing the miniature horse as a distinct breed of horse.

In 1978 the American Miniature Horse Association (AMHA) officially established the "Miniature Horse" as a separate breed. There are a lot of United States miniature horse registries and others worldwide but the AMHA is credited with establishing the American Miniature Horse breed, as a separate breed. The AMHA was formed with the intent to maintain a registry and stud book plus to adopt a standard of perfection for the breed. Today, they are considered the world's largest miniature horse registry, with nearly 140,000 registered horses in 30 countries and provinces around the world.

The AMHA suggests that if a person were to see a picture of a miniature horse, with no references whatsoever, it would be identical in proportion, conformation and characteristic wise to a full-size horse. Also, according to the AMHR a "miniature should be a small, sound, well-balanced horse and should give the impression of strength, agility and alertness. A miniature should be eager and friendly but not skittish in disposition."

CHAPTER 2: KNOWING YOUR MINIATURE HORSE

KNOWING YOUR MINIATURE HORSE:

There are many types of horse breeds such as the Percheron, Thoroughbred, French Saddle Horse, Przewalski, Camargue, Appaloosa, Pinto, Shire, Shetland Pony, Falabella and of course, the Miniature Horse. The miniature horse is the smallest in size, proportion and conformation, out of all of them. They are a very unique size but resemble their larger counterpart, the full-size horse. There is no difference between the miniature horse and the full-size horse but their smaller size. If you compare them, that's what you would see as being the difference between them.

Miniature horses were bred down from regular sized horses. They are not considered a pony and that's an insult if said to any miniature horse owner. They are actually sized down with the same characteristics of the full-sized horse.

A miniature horse must be up to 34 inches and not over to be considered a miniature horse. If over that size, than they are considered oversized. This is measured from the last hair of the withers, from the bottom of its mane, in laymen's terms. The average height is 7 to 8 hands on these miniature horses.

They range in many types of colors such as white, roan, pinto, palomino, perlino, grullo, dun, grey, cremello, chestnut, bay, black, buckskin, and champagne.

Miniature horses are friendly and interact great with people. This is one reason that they make good pets.

Miniature horses also have the same behaviors as full-sized horses. They must also be treated like equines. They are friendly, out-going, loving and caring of children and adults. They don't usually have much of a mean streak and this is why they make such good pets for children to handle them.

Small children 5 years old and younger can ride on them with assistance. A small saddle is used and an adult can walk them around on them.

They are perfect for children with supervision, of course.

These miniature horses can be breed for fun or for the purpose of selling them to other farms or people interested in getting into the miniature horse field also.

A newborn foal is a foal that was just born. A foal is a baby horse under a year old. A yearling is a horse that is a year old. A colt is a younger male horse. A filly is a younger female horse. A mare is an older female horse and a stallion is an older male horse.

When you have the birth of a colt, you must start deciding if he will grow into a stallion or will be gelded. You can check his bloodlines and see if they are great ones for breeding or if you just don't want any breeding in your barn, then you may decide to do the gelding. The gelded horse is a very gentle horse that you won't have to worry about being around your mares or broodmares. They will be a much calmer version of your colt or stallion. They are a great alternative show- wise. You can let a child care for a gelded horse without the worries of them getting hurt. They can also show these horses in the show arena for you and your family with no worries. You have to make this decision for you and your farm, deciding what's best for you. It just makes sense for some to do this procedure and geld their colts or stallions.

A gelding is a stallion or colt that has been gelded and is not able to produce babies anymore. They are much calmer than a stallion and it is a good idea to geld a horse if you do not plan on using him to breed your broodmares or for breeding purposes.

Most live on an average longer than some full-sized horse breeds. The life span for this breed of horse is often anywhere from 25 to 35 years old. And we do have some at one of our farms who are close to 25 years old now.

The miniature horse's body is made up of the same skeleton and muscular parts that a full-size horse is made up of. The only difference is their size being scaled down from them. The skeleton is made up of a skull, spine, femur, knee, ribs, and fetlock. Other than that their proportions, characteristics and conformation are all the same as the full-sized horse. The breed is no different other than their size.

The miniature horse can be shown at shows specializing in the miniature horse breed. They can be shown by leash at a walk, trot or gallop and also by carts ridden by participants. There are jumper classes where the horses jump over jumps with the participant leading them. They also have a dressage class which judge their grace, agility and obedience. There are many different classes for them to participate in. Ribbons, prizes even including money prizes are given out for these shows. There are different levels and ages of participants.

Your horse must be registered with the organizations and for the shows. Registration for the AMHA is usually done shortly after birth. A picture of the horse is taken plus the sire and mare that produced the offspring is listed, as to see the bloodlines of the horse involved.

The bloodlines of the horses are important as well because many great horses with excellent physical characteristics come from many of the most wanted horse bloodlines.

Miniature horses also have gaits. This is the way the horse moves. Wild horses move at their own pace and only have two gaits. Domestic horses are trained a bit differently and they perform at least four types of different gaits.

Miniature horses can give birth just the way the full-size horses do. The mares are extremely protective of their offspring. They will attack other horses with biting to alert them to go away from their babies. I will talk about the more later on in another chapter.

Miniature horses just as full-sized horses communicate through body language with each other. They are sensitive and clever in their mannerisms. They are sociable animals and they do prefer to live in large groups called herds. You will notice which ones get along and which ones don't just like human beings they don't all get along. So, you will notice certain ones in the field hanging around with other ones that they enjoy their company.

They can walk, trot, cantor and gallop. The walk is the slowest gait. The trot is faster than the walk but has a two-beat rhythm. The cantor is faster and has a three-beat rhythm while the gallop being the fastest with longer strides. They also get all four feet suspended in the air. This is the most exciting gait they have.

The miniature horse or full-size horses have changed over millions of years to become what we know today. They changed to become better suited to their environment. This is called the evolution of the horse, in general.

The miniature horse should have the same well-balanced, correct conformation seen in the full-sized horse breed. Stallions should be bold and masculine and mares should be refined and feminine. The idea with the miniature horse was the smallest most correct conformation wise horse you could find.

Miniature horses should be well proportioned with the head in proportion to the body and also the neck. The forehead should be broad with prominent large widely spaced eyes. The ears should be medium sized and pointed. The body should be smooth and well muscled, the back should be short and the barrel should be trim, as well. They have well muscled hips and the highest point of the croup should be even with the withers. Also, the tail should be smoothly round off the hind-end. Lastly, the legs should be straight and parallel and the hooves should be round and compact.

The smallest miniature horse in recorded history is a miniature horse stallion named "Little Pumpkin." He resided at Del Tera Miniature Horse Farm in South Caroline. He is recorded as the smallest miniature horse. He stood 14 inches tall and weighed 20 lbs. Other records indicate another horse, Black Beauty, as the smallest in the Guinness Book of World Records at 18.5 inches tall.

The smallest breeding stallion was named Bond Tiny Tim that's listed in the AMHA record books. He was only 19 inches tall. He was also a dwarf miniature horse though. He appears in many pedigrees of hundreds of miniature horses in the United States of America. He has sired many national champions and has sired many horses.

The oldest living miniature horse was recorded at over 50 years of age in North Carolina. This horse was named Angel and was a dwarf miniature horse.

These horses commonly live to be 25 to 35 years old, and horses' ages do translate into human years but with differences in age equivalents. As babies they mature at a rate much faster than human babies do. They reach their puberty at the age of two years old. Miniature horses live one third longer than the larger horse breed does. This is due to size differences. It's like a Rottweiler can live to almost 14 or so while a

Chihuahua or other smaller dog may live to 20 years old. So, it's very likely due to their size that they do live longer than the full-sized horse breed.

Knowing your miniature horse well is the key to succeeding with communication for training, exercise and showing.

Sometimes it's a good idea to be on your horse's level to get your message across or to calm them down.

Knowing your horse well takes time and patience but will pay off well, in the end.

Your miniature horse will respond better to a more calmer approach. Getting fully aquainted with your miniature horse and knowing him or her well, will help both of you to be more comfortable around one another.

All miniatures must be 34 inches or less in height. If your horse is comfortable with you, than it will have no problem with you unexpectedly touching its back half.

This is a miniature horse in the wintertime with a full coat but a clipped head.

Miniatures are great with kids holding on to them, with supervision.

Miniature horses are safe to have around small children but always with supervision for them.

CHAPTER 3: FEEDING AND GROOMING YOUR MINIATURE HORSE

FEEDING YOUR MINIATURE HORSE

Miniature horses eat the same things the larger breed eats, just in smaller portions. The eat grasses, grains and types of hay. They can also have snacks of carrots and apples plus there are horse treats available which is much similar to dog treats.

Mini horses can survive on lush grass and make excellent lawn mowers, as well. When grass is unavailable to them hay makes a great substitute, but both can be used and often are.

A small quantity of crimped oats completes their daily nutritional regimen.

Also, used daily for a source to their nutritional needs would be salt and trace minerals. An easy way to provide this is to provide the miniature horse with a brick of salt and a brick of trace mineral salt too.

Miniature horses should also always be provided with clean cool water for drinking.

Vitamin E is required for all animals and humans. It is known for its antioxidant properties. In the recent years more attention has been paid in the need for your miniature horse to have this. Vitamin E is found in green grassy pastures, so make sure your horse has plenty of that, as well. It is also found in alfalfa too. It is found in the oils of corn and soybean and other feeds. It is also found in wheat germ, which you can feed your horse. Vitamin E's main function is to protect cells from peroxidative damage. So, it has received lots of attention from owners with performance horses.

All types of horses are vegetarian and have adapted to making the most of low-grade food, mainly grass. The nutrients in grass are difficult for an animal's body to extract. But the horse breed has solved this problem by having an extra-long digestive system, and by pushing as much food as they can through their bodies. The food converts to energy in as short a time as possible. It's a virtually nonstop cycle of eating, digesting and producing waste.

A slow, deliberate style of eating ensures that the food is thoroughly ground down. This means that equines must chew slowly and wash the food down with plenty of saliva, to aid in digestion.

All miniature horses also have a sweet tooth so apples can be provided for them but they also enjoy candy, soda, and breakfast cereal but this is not advised for them.

These mini horses need to be carefully watched by owners and not overfed with extra treats to control their weight. Especially, if they are show horses. Their weight is an issue to watch over through diet and exercise.

Miniature horses need to be fed twice daily as a minimum. You can increase or decrease their food according to their size. You can adjust it to their needs. If overweight smaller amounts are necessary and if underweight increase the size of their meals.

The miniature horse's nutrients requirements go up during the wintertime months. The miniature horse needs more calories to keep warm and generate heat for him or herself.

Mature horses in good condition may not need much or any grain but they do need a good pasture or hay. A little alfalfa hay can be added during the cold wintertime months. Digestion of protein creates more heat for the miniature horses and horses in general too.

You want your horse to carry adequate weight especially during the winter months without gaining too much or losing too much either. A horse with a thicker coat may look plumper or larger so be careful to investigate it by looking over the horse. They may actually look bigger to the eye than they actually are. So, just be sure to check it out closely as not to over or under feed your miniature horse.

No matter what make sure to feed them twice a day but adjust it according to your horse's size.

GROOMING YOUR MINIATURE HORSE

Grooming is not only important on a regular basis but it's one of the most important aspects of competition, as well.

Grooming provides a valuable insight into what mood your horse is in before exercise or training.

Grooming is and can be a wonderful bonding time for your miniature horse and you.

It's a good idea to groom your miniature horse daily to keep the dust, dirt and weather elements out of their manes and coats.

In order to keep the miniature horse's coat clean, it must be groomed regularly.

Grooming also gives your horse the opportunity to get used to your touch, as well.

Invest in quality tools for the grooming of your miniature horse. Good tools may cost a little more in your budget but in the long run they will last you much longer than going the cheaper route on this one.

The size and design of the tools you use is important. If the tool you choose to use is not comfortable chances are you won't use it to groom regularly. There are brands out there that are made for women to use. They fit better in the woman's hand. Understand that some horses may need a stiffer comb or brush and others may need a softer one. Plus, the pressure of your brushing may vary as well. Take extra care with the mane and tail. Find a routine with this that suits both you and the style of the horse. Each horse is going to respond differently to the methods used.

Also, keep your tools very clean. Clean brushes monthly with very mild dish soap and rinse them very well too also place them bristle side down to dry off. Because you will use them on your horse's body use a mild soap or natural soap product to clean them. You should also consider cleaning or washing your harness on a weekly basis.

Developing a good routine will be the best thing for both your horse and you. Everything starts from the inside out with the health of your horse but grooming and keeping your horse clean will make your miniature horse feel wonderful.

In the hotter months you will want to clip down the coat of the miniature horse so they won't be so hot. Plus, if showing them this is the norm for that. There coats tend to grow thick winter coats. It makes the horse more comfortable in the hotter months. Also, heavy sweating under the thick hair may cause the animal to lose weight and exposes it to the risk of a chill, as well. Some hair on the miniature horse will shed on its own but it's a very slow process so it helps to clip them.

During the colder months you may want to only wash their legs off, if it's too cold to fully bathe them. Then just use your currycomb to keep the winter coat from getting to dirty and grungy. Also, a damp cloth works well for sweat, the face, ears and eyes to keep them clean as well.

Clipping your miniature horse for the first time will likely be an experience you won't soon forget. Your miniature horse may not like the sound of the buzzing of the clippers. The horse will not be used to it but over time will get use to it. It's wise to tie your horse up or do it in there stall tied up. It's probably a wise decision to have someone with experience help show you the way with this the first time, until you get the hang of it.

For an unruly horse you may want to use a twitch, which is placed on the horses' upper lip. The clippers do become hot so be careful. You can stop until the clipper heads become cooler during the clipping process. You can also dip the blades in kerosene every five minutes and that will keep the machine from getting too hot plus the blades sharpened.

It's advisable to do the horse's head and face first before they get too unruly. The buzzing sound is likely to annoy your horse. You may want to start with less sensitive areas behind the head and on the neck then move your way up to the head after that. Set aside an hour or more for the process of clipping the miniature horse. You want to take your time with this, as it will come out better that way. You can provide a blanket if it's still chilly out. That will help keep the miniature horse warmer when not doing any exercises.

The miniature horse, as does any other horse, needs to have its hooves clipped also. This can be done by you but is usually done by a professional. They can also correct any problems the horse may have with how its conformation is. It's a very useful practice for show horses and all other types of horses.

The grooming of the horse also relieves any itching they may have.

You can use a currycomb made of metal to clean out the regular brush you use freeing it of dirt and hair from your horse. But you can use the currycomb as well just be gentle with it. Once the coat becomes sleek the brush will then be enough.

Before brushing your horse, stand where the horse can see you. Now let the horse sniff the comb or brush becoming familiar with it. Then stand by the horse's side and start brushing the front parts of its body. The proper method of brushing the miniature horse is to go with the hair, never against it. You'll notice the interesting patterns of how the hair grows; then go with the hair. When doing the back parts of the horse please do not stand directly behind the horse. You don't want to accidentally get kicked plus it's easier on the horse if it can see you. The horse may get startled otherwise.

At first your horse may not like getting its legs brushed. Go down them with your hands first, then gently with the brush to do them.

Your miniature horses' mane has a natural tendency to fall either to the left of the right side, but if neglected it will be divided between the sides. You can train it to go to one side or the other though. You may have to wet down the unruly locks of hair to one side or the other daily to get it to stay there. Don't hesitate to brush vigorously. There are no pain nerves in the base of the horse's neck, so it doesn't seem to bother them and they do seem to enjoy this, as well. Some trainers even pull some of the hairs out in the manes and tails to make them look better for showing. This doesn't seem to bother them either. You will notice after awhile that your miniature horse enjoys this daily activity with you by its side.

Bathing the horse at times is a definite necessity. It's up to you how often you choose to do this. As long as the horse's coat doesn't dry out it's fine to do. There is no substitute for good grooming for your horse. Using clean water and a good body wash will do no harm to your horse. But there are many shampoos out there made for horses but any will do.

Horses do get stained and dirty. It's important to do the bathing a few days before shows so the horse can regain his gloss back. You should only wash a horse if it's quite warm or if you have a heated barn for them to dry in. To wash him you'll need warm water, a sponge, a currycomb and some good old patience. Just go slow with the horse. Some even like this process or get use to it after the first few times. The bath will also help in keeping your horses hooves moistened.

It is important to have good grooming tools. The saying "A workman is only as good as his tools" is very true in this case. Especially when grooming is done for the miniature horse that is being shown. The basic grooming tools are the currycomb, dandy (stiff) brush, hoof pick, the body brush which would be soft, a sponge and a scraper for drying your miniature horses. Also an ordinary plastic hairbrush can be used and a metal mane or tail comb, as well. Turkish towels make good rags for rubbing their coats also. You can also buy a kit or container to keep track of all your tools or have a special place for them, in your barn where you can easily reach or get to them.

Grooming is an important part of your daily activities. It not only keeps up the appearance of your miniature horse but it is also good for their health. It massages the skin and underlying muscles, which promotes local blood circulation and healthy growth of hair. It also gives you the opportunity to examine the horse closely, as well.

A miniature horse can have the mane and tail braided for horse shows you go to or just for fun. They seem to love any extra attention you give them when grooming them and they also look just beautiful with either a nicely combed or brushed out tail or one with many bows or ribbons braided for whatever the occasion. It's up to you what you do with it but just something extra to keep in mind.

Also, make sure you have a nice secure stall for your miniature horse. It should be cleaned out daily of manure and urine. It also needs a bed of shavings for them to lie down on. Lime can be used underneath to keep the excess urine from smelling up the stall. They like to have a nice clean stall to eat and sleep in. Make sure to have a safe secure door to prevent the horse from escaping.

Also, they like the perimeters of the stall to be sized down to their size so they can see out of them, at least at where the gate in the front of it is. This also enables them to hair airflow, as well. They enjoy seeing the surroundings and other horses or animals you may have, while in there. A very small space is required for them to thrive in, that's one reason they make for great pets or show horses.

Fencing outside should be done with wood not chain link fence. Chain link fence is not a good idea. Stallions must be separated from mares or they will breed without you knowing. So, keep this is mind if you get more than one miniature horse. Many two year old fillies have had babies because no one though the yearlings were old enough to breed successfully. You don't want any unexpected babies. The pregnancies have to be closely monitored throughout their cycle.

Also, some stallions do get along with gelded miniature horses, so you may be able to place them in pens together outside. But it's all trial and error as to who will get along with one another. So, just be aware that with more horses also makes for more pens and the responsibilities that come along with that aspect.

DAILY ROUTINES

- Start with a soft bristle brush on the miniature horse's face. Don't use a regular brush, as they are too hard for their faces. Save that for the legs and body.
- Moisten a washcloth and gently rub the places that need attention on the horse's eyes and face.
- Then gently brush on the forelock, the mane and also the tail using a pincushion type of hairbrush. You can start from the bottom of the

tail and work your way up it. This method breaks the fewest numbers of their hair in the tail. Horses need their tails to keep the pesky flies and bugs away from them. They use them to swat and keep them away from them.

- Now comes a combination technique. It takes some practice but you can learn how to do this. Use circular motions with a soft rubber currycomb in one hand, following with a regular bristle body brush in the other to wipe away any of the dust and/or hair. Be gentle on the girth area and under the belly as these are more sensitive areas for the miniature horse or any horses for that fact.

- Finally, make sure to clean out under the feet and hooves. Then you're ready to go and your horse will not only be a very happy one but also a clean one, as well.

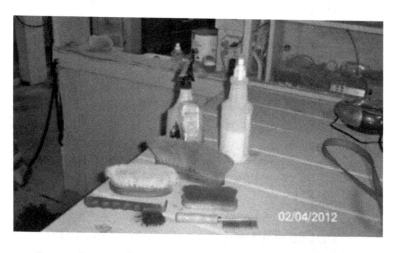

Grooming tools are necessary for your miniature horse. Here are just a few of them: Brushes, currycomb, regular comb, face brush, laser sheen, fly spray, hoof pick and a lead to tie them with.

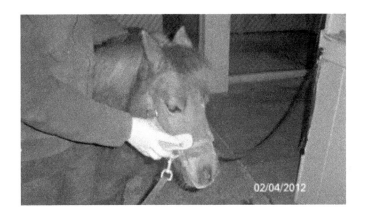

Brushing your horse with a softer smaller face brush is important for the daily cleaning of your miniature horses.

Brushing your horse thoroughly with a brush on its body, neck and tail, is part of the daily grooming, for your miniature horse.

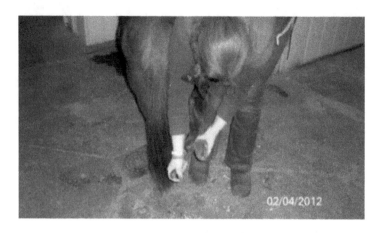

It's a good idea to keep your miniature horse's hooves cleaned and picked out by using a horse pick on them. You start from the back of the hoof and go down or top to bottom by positioning yourself like this picture shows.

Knowing how much your miniature horse needs to eat is very important, to maintain the right healthy weight.

CHAPTER 4: BREEDING, PREGNANCY AND FOALING

BREEDING

With miniature horses this is more of a science because it's usually handled by the owner in a different manner than in the wild or naturally. Usually, the stallion is selected specifically with the bloodlines of the mares to produce the best offspring.

The stallion is usually taken to a secluded area and brought to the mare that is in heat and ready for breeding. It's charted on a calendar each time the process is done, so we have some idea of when the foal will be due.

In order to learn how to understand more about the effects of breeding decisions, you should learn to read a horse's pedigree and how to also examine the miniature horse's ancestry. Learn more about the names listed there, in other words. It will tell you a lot about your horse and its breeding background in order to know your horse's bloodlines and how well they'd do in the show arena.

When looking for a miniature horse the foal or horse you see reflects generations of ancestors. Knowing where your horse came from will better help you in the long run to determine a lot of things including any health issues that may arise also that runs in their history.

A chart called a pedigree chart is a way to trace your miniature horse's history of ancestors. The charts also include stallions for studs, miniature horses and full-sized horses for sale, in sales catalogs and also farm brochures.

The animals or miniature horse in this case is identified by a certificate or the "papers." The registry that you sign up for verifies all the information regarding the accuracy of the ancestry of your miniature horse. The chart does list two generations on both sides...the dam and sire of your horse.

Every established breed has certain famous bloodlines and you will begin to recognize them in time, when you have been in this business a while.

Basically this pedigree chart is a family tree of your miniature horse. But it becomes very important when showing your horse, if the bloodlines are good ones.

PREGNANCY AND FOALING

Most people never intended to have many miniature horses but they are addictive. The average number owned is around eight horses. Most were not even horse people until they bought a miniature horse. Many of first time owners have accidental births the first time as they were not being careful with their stallions and mares.

The gestation time is 330 days but they can come as early as 300 days. Some mares will foal in ten months and then some miniature horse mares will decide to go a full twelve months. That's why they need to be carefully monitored, in case of a problem with their delivery of the baby foal. The foaling characteristics of the mare will probably continue with each birth.

As expected with premature foals, they will likely be very small and delicate requiring extra attention from you and its mother. While the 12 month old foal may be born measuring 23 inches instead of the average norm of 18 inches at birth. This horse may be more advanced for its age as well. Also, the ten month old foal and the 12 month old foal could very well come out the same size.

A miniature horse is pregnant for around 11 months. During that time she goes through a normal pregnancy, hopefully with no complications while growing in size comfortably. Only one foal is usually the norm for horses.

The birth of the horse only takes several minutes if all goes well. The mare usually lies on her side to give birth but could also do it standing in an upright position. The foal will usually emerge head first. It will still have its caul covering it that it was in the womb in during the pregnancy. It soon breaks free from this caul, shakes itself off and tries to stand for the first time.

The placenta through which food was received comes out immediately after birth. The mother might chew on this but won't eat it. The mother licks the baby foal all over especially under the tail to stimulate its first feces. Plus, licking establishing the first bonding of the mother miniature horse to her new baby. From now on the mother will be able to recognize her foal. There bond is one that won't be broken and the mother becomes very protective of her offspring.

Foals can be born in any month of the year, but under natural conditions most miniature horses will be born from March through June. This is because the miniature horse mares cycles normally in the north hemisphere during the springtime and early summertime months. The heat cycle depends on the light and how many hours of it they have which can be natural or artificial.

The highest rates for conception in miniature horses and horses are recorded in April through July in the United States of America. Therefore the birthing would be from March to June of the next year. The reproductive process is from the months of February to March for the miniature horse.

Acceptance of the stallion for breeding by the mare is when the mares begin to cycle normally and is a fertile time for them. Their heat or season only occurs every 21 days that is their cycle for miniature horses. Most of the mares stay in heat from five to seven days and will also come into heat or season five to seven days after foaling, as well. This is called the "foal heat." For conception to happen, the male sperm must be present during the time of ovulation for pregnancy to happen.

Therefore, the timing of the breeding must be just right in mares and often very difficult. You may have to try many times before she takes and gets pregnant by the stallion. You must realize when your mare is in heat and there will be signs. She may have a shorter than usual cycle for you to catch with her in order to get her pregnant. They have many signs for you to watch for. The flapping of the tail plus the vulva will wink which is open and close. If you look under her tail you will notice this. But it will be apparent to you when you bring the stallion around her. She'll let you know if she is interested or not in him. It's very easy to tell if she is in heat or not. When not in heat she may have kicked or bite him but now she seems more interested in him.

The reproductive tract becomes a brighter red color as the circulation increased and the cervix is opened. You can tease a mare daily with a stallion or even a gelding to test the waters and see if your mare is in heat, this will detect the onset of estrus. Hopefully your stallion is there with your mare and not at someone else's farm, if that is the case, you may want to leave your mare there for a week or so during her cycle. This will ensure she gets breed with any luck. Some leave their mares for 30 to 45 days during two heat cycles. It's up to you and your breeder to decide. You will most likely have to pay for the horse stay as well. It can get a bit costly.

Many choose to pasture breed their horse also but this method is not necessarily the best. It's hard to track the time of conception. This pasture breeding is when a stallion is put out in the field with selected mares for breeding. Some stallions will reject some mares it's just something that happen. As will some mares to some stallions. Then another stallion is needed.

No matter how a mare is bred, it's important to have a plan of action ready   for her pregnancy. Keep up with her vitamins and take extra special care of her.

The mare must also be wormed regularly too. They need this quarterly where the probability of parasite contamination is great. This is a condition that exists a lot when many horses are kept in a small area year round.

Pregnancy can be determined after fourteen days by ultrasound by your vet. We had an ultrasound machine to check on our horses, which was a great asset to us but they cost a fortune. So, using the vet for this is the way to go for you. Also, they could miscarry if there were problems with the foal so this does not insure a foal every year out of every mare you have. These problems do arise but they are not setbacks but just how things go sometimes. You must keep in mind that if a mare miscarried, then there was probably something wrong with the miniature horse foal anyway. So, it's probably for the best.

Most mares will start to show in about eight months while some keep their figure a little longer but don't worry either way. Also, udder development will be apparent about four weeks before they foal. This will give you a good idea that the foal will be coming in about a month or so. During the last week the foal will drop in the mare's abdomen. Also, changes in the mare will be apparent to you. About 48 to 72 hours prior to birth the mare's utters will start dripping milk. The dripping milk is actually colostrum which the baby needs to drink after birth. The colostrum will actually harden on the teats and this is known as "waxing over."

In the last 24 hours before foaling the mare will show signs of distress. You may notice her staying away from the other miniature horses. She may be biting at her sides, paw, lay down and getting up frequently, whether she is in a paddock or in her stall. She should be put in a stall that is adequate in size for her, at least an 8' by 8' one at nighttime would be good for her. She must be observed by you. The stall should not be over bedded but soft bedding can prevent the sac from tearing away from the new arrival. It can be dangerous to have sawdust or shavings to the mother and the new miniature horse foal. Human company during foaling is usually what the mother likes also. Many have left for fifteen minutes and come back to a new foal trying to get to its feet.

The actual birth process should take about twenty minutes with no complications arising but some are as few as five minutes. If the birth is a normal one as we all hope for than a balloon-like membrane will first appear from the mare. That will next break and about a half gallon of fluid will come out of that. After a few minutes a forefoot should appear, then the front of the hoof, then the other forefoot. The way this happens means that only one shoulder will be passing through at a time through the cervix, which definitely makes it easier on the mare during birthing out her new foal.

Next the head will appear, after the shoulders have come through. It will come out tucked in between the forelegs. After the shoulders and head are through, the rest comes through rather quickly. The birthing track is circular and down so any assistance given to the mini mare should be within that track. Please don't ever try to pull a foal up or straight out and definitely don't use a calf-puller or any other traction device on the mare.

If the mare has any difficulties in her birth of her new foal please call your veterinarian immediately. Any delays may risk losing the miniature horse mare or her foal.

If the birth of your new miniature horse foal goes well, then the foal will be on the ground with the umbilical cord attached to it. The foal's head should be free of the sac and breathing on its own. If this is the case and the foal is still receiving blood from the umbilical cord to the placenta, then leave them be. If the foal's nostrils are not clear of the sac then please tear it open so she or he can breathe.

In about five to ten minutes your baby foal will try to stand. Let him or her do this on their own. They will struggle but then succeed when they are ready to. This is all very normal for the foal to do and doesn't take too long to do. Eventually the umbilical cord will break free. Save the placenta for your vet to look over as well. If the placenta isn't expelled after four hours also call your vet for that too. Please disinfect the foal's umbilical cord with some iodine or other prescribed disinfectant.

After the new foal tries to stand and bond with its mother within two hours it should begin trying to nurse sometimes much sooner than that. It's important for them to nurse in the first 24 hours especially, because this gives them the necessary colostrums from their mother. It contains antibodies that are good for them. Nature will take care of everything for mother and baby.

But some first time mothers may need some assistance especially with getting the baby foal to nurse from them. Some babies just can't get to the mother's teats on their own but once they do they can find it after that. It's best if the mother mare and baby are left alone in the first twenty four hours or so as other mares may try to steal her baby at first.

Also, the mother miniature horse mare, takes in the scent of her new baby foal. Once she does that she will always know this is her foal and not one of the other mares with her. The horses have a great sense of smell and the different smells tell them a lot about one another.

Broodmare owners don't like to hear the word C-section when it comes to their foaling season but sometimes in order to save mare and/or foal it is necessary to do. Yes, even with miniature horses we are making great advances in the care and treatment of our miniature horses. It does typically mean a large vet bill and it does usually but not always mean losing the foal during the process. But sometimes it's the only option you have as a miniature horse owner.

There are tell-tale signs usually that the mare will have trouble delivering the foal the natural way. Sometimes she is too narrow in her hips or if she is round or flat at the end of her croup which typically will signal a more narrow pelvis in your miniature horse. If you stand behind your miniature horse mare and look down from the rump down her tail you will usually be able to tell this. The area is more triangular shaped then the normal round shape on the mare horse. The height of the horse doesn't seem to factor into this though. A C-section performed on a miniature horse is most likely the last resort to save at least the mare and if able to the foal, as well. This C-section procedure is not performed a lot. It's usually only requested to be performed by the rich and the famous.

Just because this is performed once on a mini mare horse doesn't necessarily mean she can't have normal deliveries and births the next times. It's not hard to find a vet who can do this procedure but finding one who can do it the right way might be the problem. That's why it's important to make sure that you get the best vet you can find to start out with. This is someone you will need a lot to keep your horse in tip top shape, at all times. So, make sure that you choose your vet wisely, when looking for one.

Foals are great fun for everyone and come in many different colors. They range anywhere from 15 inches to 20 inches in height when born.

They can be trained to lie across your body when they are very young or just hang out with you and their mother.

Foals enjoy each other for playing and socializing when young and usually remain friends throughout their lives.

The mother mare's are very protective of their offspring and will fight other mares that come too close to them.

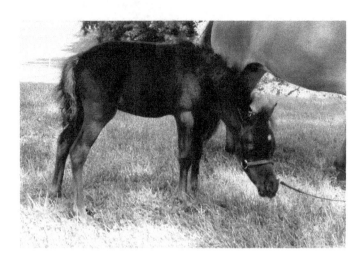

Miniature horse mares bond quickly with their young babies and remain close for quite sometime.

Mares bond very quickly with their babies, after their birth by nuzzling and trying to get them to nurse or eat from them.

Mother mares or broodmares love to graze with their babies. They are inseperable when they are out together.

Miniature horse mothers and their offspring often play together most of the day between naps.

CHAPTER 5: SICKNESS AND CHOOSING A VETERINARIAN

SICKNESS

Miniature horses are generally healthy but your miniature horse may get sick and you should be aware of signs of sickness or illness with your horse. Maybe what you think is bad behavior is your horse letting you know they are not feeling well. Your miniature horse is probably healthy if you don't notice anything wrong with it but it acts sicker than humans when it has only a small stomachache.

The most common illness or sickness that your miniature horse can have is called colic. Colic is a severe stomachache or irritated intestines. Horses can't vomit due to how their bodies are built. They have a one way digestive system. This is very dangerous to them but this is how their bodies are made. So, this is why they get severe colic. Please be careful to watch out for the signs of this illness for them. Signs or symptoms of colic would be frequently getting up and lying down, continued rolling, looking back at or biting itself, and stretching unusually often. If this occurs it's important to call the vet as soon as possible so he can diagnose this and medicate the horse for this. It can become very serious if it goes untreated.

Colic in the pregnant mare is a definite emergency and the vet should be called immediately. Even if she survives it the baby foal may not be able to. The loss of the fetus is the main concern with colic in the pregnant miniature horse broodmare. As I said this is not something to fool around with and you should call your vet immediately and seek professional help right away with this illness.

An indication of a cold, influenza or distemper would be coughing, shivering, nasal discharge and/or refusal to eat. Again calling the vet is advised for this also.

If you notice watering of the eye or a discoloring of the eye or eyes than it is most likely an eye infection or eye trouble of some sore and again this is something the vet can give you medications for. In the meantime, just wash the eye with a soft cloth and some warm water.

Infections are any discharges from any wounds or areas. Seek vet help for any of these types of sicknesses.

If your miniature horse should faint it is due to heat or a severe brain disorder. Please call your vet immediately.

Swaying can be the cause of severe kidney trouble or food poisoning. Please seek medical attention for this, as well.

Offensive smell or diarrhea is caused by spoiled food or irritated intestines.

Limping is caused by an injury to the hoof or leg trouble.

Falling hair is caused by poor conditions, mange or lice. It can be treated with shampoos some of these conditions and should be tending to immediately.

A loss of appetite is caused by a combination of other symptoms and can indicate numerous types of illnesses or sicknesses. The miniature horse should be watched carefully if it's refusing to eat. This is a sign for many, many things and not to be taken lightly.

One of your greatest assets to your miniature horse is a good veterinarian. Aside from the emergency help he or she will give, your horse will also be immunized against getting many diseases that can be stopped. This is a great preventive measure to take with your miniature horse. This keeps your horse in tip top shape and alleviates some of your worries. The vaccinations are a great help also.

Also, your vet can detect problems that you may not be aware of. It may take several hours for your vet to get there. You may want to ask him for some supplies and medications to have on hand for these emergency times and for general use, as well. If it's a minor situation with your mini horse then you can treat the horse yourself. But when in doubt also seek professional help from your vet. The vet can usually tell if it's an emergency or not and whether you need him or her to come over and check out your horse for you.

First Aid for your miniature horse is a great knowledge to have. It will help in times of emergency when waiting for you vet to be there.

FIRST AID TIPS

- Burns: cut off the hair and apply cannic acid jelly dissolved in the water to form a coating over the burned area.
- Colic: you want to ease the bellyache your miniature horse has developed. The horse may lie down, frequently roll, and refuse to eat any food. Try to keep the horse from lying down, as it may break or twist its gut. Force it to get on its feet and keep leading it around if you have to until your vet arrives to aid you with this.
- Constipation: If your horse has good grass, hay, water, and salt and gets plenty of exercise outside it should not have much trouble with constipation but you could ask your vet what medication can be given for this also. Usually what humans use would be the same in this situation but it's best to get it from the vet.
- Cough: You can cover your miniature horse with blankets to keep it warm. Feed it some moistened hay, boiled oats, linseed mash or fresh grass. A chronic cough may be heaves. But this is something to discuss with the vet, as well.
- Diarrhea: This may be caused by poor teeth, spoiled or musty foods, or other causes may be the culprit. Feed hay instead of grass for a day or so. You could also add a handful of flour to the grain as well. But there are also medications out there for this too. Get direction on this from your vet.
- Eye trouble: Bathe the eye with a warm boric acid solution and keep an eye on it. No pun intended.

- Heaves: Beginning heaves may cause coughing, which is can be caused after exercise when drinking and eating hay or grain as well. This is a chronic lung condition and requires special attention in feeding also with the care of the horse. Consult your vet on how to handle this problem.
- Lice: To rid the horse of lice, you must clip them and then wash them with a weak Lysol solution. If the weather outside is cold then make sure to use a blanket on your miniature horse. The lice will not pass to humans and you must disinfect the blanket as well, if you had been using it while the infection existed.
- Puncture around the foot: This could be serious in nature so please call your vet. They may want to give your horse an anti-tetanus injection.
- Skin Disease: Lumps, sores, pimples, itching, and bare spots have many causes and all require different types of treatments. An itching tail may be caused by pin worms. Call you vet for his or her opinion with these matters.
- Nosebleeds: If there is a broken vessel which causes the bleeding it will usually repair itself. Do not plug up the nostrils because horses cannot breathe through their mouths. Apply a cold compress to the outside area of the nose. You can also syringe a little cold water up the nostrils and add calcium lactate to the food.
- Swaying: This is an indication of food poisoning or bad kidneys if your horse's hindquarters begin to sway. Remove any tack on the horse and make the horse more

comfortable. Call your vet right away or your horse may not survive this. There is no more you can do on your own with this swaying.

- Swelling: Any unusually swelling of any areas can indicate many many things so contact your vet and get his or her advice on this symptom.
- Worms: Your horse will not thrive at all with this condition. He may be thin and listless with this illness. He will rub his tail and stretch his neck up. There are several things to do to keep him or her relatively worm free. Never make him eat anything with manure on it. Remove all manure daily to prevent this from happening.
- Respiratory health: In the winter time if a horse is confined to a barn the horse is at risk for respiratory health problems. Heaves are the most common respiratory health issue for the miniature horse. It can also be caused by dusty hay.

Heaves can be characterized by a chronic cough, labored breathing, lack of stamina, weight loss, lack of response to antibiotics or sometimes a watery discharge from the miniature horse's nostrils. It is most common among the adult miniature horses.

The breathing difficulty is due to swelling that narrows the air passages and inflammation, as well. Heaves is a forced effort to exhale, sometimes also known as double expiration. Air can be drawn in easily but the horse is having trouble pushing it out. This puts a strain on their abdomens during this time.

It takes weeks for the inflammation to disappear. The horse can relapse if put back in the barn and this was due to dust and spores. A horse with this problem must be watched carefully and protected from this environment as much as possible, in order to recuperate from it. Once a horse develops this he must be in a dust free environment especially in the wintertime.

A mash consisting of grain and molasses can be given to eliminate or reduce dustiness in it. None of these efforts will help if other horses have dusty pens with straw bedding so you'd have to have the same dust free atmosphere for all your horses to eliminate the problems with this situation.

Nature helps in giving the horse a nice warm winter coat but you must take other precautions in the wintertime to keep them warm also. Blankets are a big help and having a nice clean stall free of urine and manure with fresh bedding for them. The thicker the bedding the warmer they should stay. Never bed with dusty or moldy hay or bedding. Shavings are the best way to go with the miniature horses.

Make sure they have fresh clean water available to them also. Make sure the water is not frozen during the winter months, as well. Feeding them roughage is a good way to warm them up on early mornings when they are very cold. A pound of hay is more roughage than a pound of grain is to the miniature horse. Corn is considered a cold weather feed but this is not true. A pound of oats and hay will produce body heat for them.

Arthritis in older horses is more noticeable in the winter months for them. They cannot move fast during this time because of pain. It may be necessary to separate the older horses because of this. Weanlings need extra care also during their first wintertime also.

"Choke" is a term used by horse enthusiasts, a type of lingo to describe esophageal impaction. This can occur when a horse happens to swallow something that is too large, course or thick for them to swallow. It doesn't pass smoothly down their throat down the esophagus, from their pharynx to their stomach. It's called a feed bolus and it gets stuck at some point in their esophagus. The feed gets stuck and stops at the blockage in their esophagus. It depends on how sensitive the horse is, if he stops eating or not. If the horse continues to eat this may last for hours or days, if the owner doesn't notice the problem exists for the miniature horse.

Signs of this choke condition are sudden refusal to eat by the miniature horse, lying down on the ground, rolling in distress, stretching the head back and forth, coughing, eye rolling by the horse, pawing, etc. The sign that distinguishes the differences between colic and choke is the feed running from the horse's nostrils. This is not always apparent though. Some cases of this choke resolve themselves quickly but others may need more attention from the owner and possibly a vet, as well. Sometimes surgery may be necessary to take care of this problem. Sometimes it's not even treatable for the miniature horse.

Protect your miniature horse from EIA which is Equine Infectious Anemia. This is potentially fatal if it goes untreated. The virus causes EIA reproduces in the white blood cells of the horse that circulate throughout the body. Antibodies may attack and destroy red blood cells leading to the anemia in your horse. Horses may die as a result of this or secondary illnesses that occur due to this deadly disease.

Angular Limb Deformities, also known as ALD, can affect your miniature horses and all types of horse breeds. ALD is common in miniature horses. It is carpal joint laxity, a condition that shows up or is present in birth. It's due to a lack of surrounding soft tissue strength to support the joints. Also, there is no pain present and also the limb can be straightened by a manual method used. Exercise in the pasture can strengthen the muscle tone and tissues. But talk to your vet about the options with this disease, to find out what else can be done for it.

Miniature horses can suffer also from ulcers. Sometimes the symptoms are silent but can be deadly if they go untreated. The symptoms are often misdiagnosed with ulcers. Some symptoms are as subtle as a bad attitude or the horse acting down and out to symptoms looking as if the horse has colic. Other symptoms can also be as vague as the horse just not being its usual self or biting its side which is also a symptom of colic. They may kick at their sides, they may have depression, they may stretch when they urinate, or poor body condition or performance can be a sign of ulcers too.

Foals will show some different symptoms, as well such as a different posture lying down or getting up from the ground or lying on their backs with their feet in an upward direction. Also, they may lie on their chests instead of on their sides. It's just not that easy to detect or diagnose but it is something to know is out there in sicknesses for your miniature horse. They are painful attacks for horses to go through. Stomach ulcers are a very real threat to horses but proper management and prevention can prevent your miniature horse from getting them. This can be prevented but some horses under stress do get them and they can go undiagnosed for quite a long time.

To prevent them you must realize that stress is the number one reason why the horse gets them. Also, many activities we may do with our horses are actually stressful to them. Try to avoid any changes in the horse's daily routine or activities you have for them and limit stall confinement also. Allow the horse additional time to settle into new surroundings like show areas for example, Limit the use of Bute and Bonamine, which are bad for the stomach lining. Also, avoid sweet feed like ones with molasses or acids, which are not good for the stomach. Wean foals together to alleviate some of the stress involved in it. Offer food and water to the horse when transporting it. And lastly, give down time to horses after training or returning from a show.

Some studies have shown that giving the horse alfalfa can coat the lining of the stomach and may prevent some ulcers from happening to your miniature horse. What you would do is feed a small amount of alfalfa about 30 minutes or so before you exercise your horse. This gives the alfalfa some time to reach the stomach of your horse and prevents some of the acid from doing its harm to the horse. This of course won't be of any help to an already existing ulcer; this is more a preventative measure for you to take with your miniature horse. This tends to buffer the acid in the stomach and helps to coat it.

Some substitutions that you can use are pellets or cubes of alfalfa, a high-calcium fiber source such as beet pulp can be used as well. A vet can prescribe some human medications to help your miniature horse, if he realizes there is a problem of ulcers. There are many he can prescribe to fix the illness within your miniature horse.

Horses of all types of breeds use vision with both eyes until the object is between three to four feet in front of them. Then they lower their heads down and observe things with one eye. The miniature horse's retina is adapted for the detection of movement. Cones are present in the miniature horse's retina which is supposedly suggesting that they have the capacity for color vision but only in the form of blues and reds. But this is not known for sure, it is just suggested by what we see with their eyes.

A horse has a total vision field of 360 degrees. This does mean that the horse can see its tail while looking in front of him or her.

In foals there can be ocular problems concerning their eyes. A new foal can develop droopy eyelids, a round pupil, low tear secretions, reduced sensitivity or lack of reflexes for up to two weeks or more after birth.

Enropion is the inward rolling of the eyelid margin on the baby foal. This can cause the eyelid hairs to press on the cornea. It can be a problem with foals or even secondary to emaciation or dehydration as in "downer foals." Sutures can be placed in the lid margin to roll out the affected eyelid or eyelids.

Microphithalinus is a small eye and is common as a congenital defect in some mini foals. Some lesions may be present also. This may be a visual problem or one that can cause blindness in your miniature horse foal.

Iridocyclitis in a foal is generally secondary to a severe illness in your miniature horse. This may occur in one or both of your horse's eyes. Red cells, white cells and proteins may be present.

Lid trauma in your miniature horse foals need to be corrected with some kind of surgery. Eyelids have a great capacity to heal after the surgery too.

Eyelid melanomas are found a lot in grey horses. Melanomas may be singular or multiple. The treatment is a surgical one of excisions, and also cryotherapy may help.

Sarcoids are solitary or also multiple tumors present in the eyelids and perocular regions of the horse.

Also, there is something called separation anxiety in a horse. This isn't exactly a sickness or an illness but more like depression in a horse. This can sometimes be dangerous to the mini horse or the owners. This is a common condition with horses throughout their lives. In every horse's life some sort of separation occurs and devastates the horse for a while, causing anxiety and depression with the horse.

The horse enjoys the company of another horse or a previous owner that had to get rid of him and thus, this is the start of it. This is usually traumatic to the horse although we as owners don't usually realize this. The horse is actually a highly social animal and enjoys being around other horses, so this all does make sense if you think about it. Separation in horses is more about survival and instinct than simple a desire to be around other horses.

Most horses and miniature horses do enjoy the company of other equine to be around them. Any horse or animal is capable of experiencing separation anxiety. It's just like when you have more than one pet around one another and then one passes away, you will notice the remaining animals are depressed and down for awhile after their passing. It's just the same as with humans they go through a mourning period when another animal in their lives is gone. But the process for them is usually short lived and they will move on soon with things.

A foal has an inefficient immune system at birth and is sometimes not able to fight off infectious organisms, which include bacteria, fungus, virus and parasites that bombard the mini horse foal at birth. The passive transfer of antibodies that the foal receives from its mini mother by way of the colostrum milk provided by her. This is the principle protection that a foal does receive from the mother.

Sometimes it fails to receive enough protection from the mother causing it to suffer from different illnesses. This passage transfer is the single one most life-threatening thing to suffer from with a newborn foal. The newborn foal needs to receive the initial milk containing the colostrum when it is first born to gain the great benefits from that first milk. It must do this early on while that type of milk is available to him or her, right after the newborn foal's birth.

CHOOSING A VETERINARIAN

Horses seldom come with a money-back guarantee and they are a big investment not only with time but also with your emotions. So, choosing the right vet to help in the care of your horse is a big deal. It should not go lightly. You should investigate and look into the vet that will be taking care of your horse for you. It's a very important aspect of owning your new miniature horse.

Make sure before you purchase your horse you check on your horse's overall health and also its condition before you make this investment. It's the best thing to do to protect yourself and know that you are getting a horse that will be around for a long time, one with no health issues.

It doesn't matter if you want only a pet quality horse or one for showing around the country; you want to make sure that all is well health-wise with this miniature horse.

Purchase examinations on your horse may vary. It depends on what you are getting the horse for. It requires good communication between yourself and your vet, as well. So, take your time in finding the right vet for this job of taking care of your miniature horse. It's nice to have someone you feel comfortable in speaking with and dealing with. You will be seeing a lot of this vet so this is so important right from the start.

Choose a vet who is familiar with this breed of horse, the miniature horse.

Also, explain to your vet all the expectations you may have and what you expect from this relationship. Try to include your long term and short term expectations or goals with this too.

Ask the vet to outline the procedures of the initial exam on your miniature horse that he feels should be included for you. Also, find out the costs for these procedures up front so you know beforehand.

Make sure you are present for this initial exam. This is the purchase exam both you and the seller or their agent should be present also.

You can also try to discuss what your vet's feelings are on the horse in private.

Definitely don't be afraid to ask the questions and request more information. This is a big investment and you don't want to make the wrong decisions about it.

The job of the vet is neither to pass it or fail the horse. It is to provide you with the best knowledge and information regarding this horse. You want to know the health and physical characteristics of this horse. It's best to go with your vet's advice and your own instincts. You know that ultimately the decision to buy is yours and no one else's. But your vet has the extra knowledge to help you with that important decision in buying your first miniature horse.

I would not buy a horse without the knowledge of at least an expertise in the field. But the purchase exam is a good way to gain a lot of knowledge that you may want to know about your horse. Also, look at their pedigrees and how their ancestors were health wise. This is a good judge by how your horse will do too.

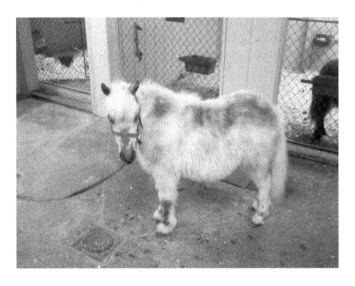

Choosing the right veterinarian will keep your horse from getting sick. This is a very important step to take, as you will have a long-term relationship with the right vet.

CHAPTER 6: ALL ABOUT STALLIONS

STALLIONS

Over history looking back through the AMHA many stallions top the charts, as the best stallions for producing World Champions consistently. Most of the historical stallions have been called the "great ones" over the years for their excellent production of foals.

It could be debated for years, as to what makes a great stallion. It's the owner, breeder and trainer who need to think that the stallion is truly great. That's what makes them one of those chart topping names in the history of the AMHA and amongst other breeders and enthusiasts.

Many stallions make a name for themselves in their own right and with their great champion offspring. One of those great named stallions would be Rowdy. Rowdy was a beautiful bay. Also, in 1984 came Lazy N Red Boy, just to mention a few. We had some offspring of Rowdy at one time.

I thought it'd be important to include a section on stallions, as they are sometimes like a different breed all together. What I mean is that having a stallion is a bit different than a mare in many ways and I think before you decide to get one, you should know all the facts or behaviors of that stallion.

For many breeders or owners their first miniature horse was a stallion. Maybe they thought they'd be getting it gelded when they bought it but then decided otherwise. Sometimes the horse just proves to be too nice and they decide to breed it. Or he was just so well-behaved that they thought it was fine not to geld the stallion. For whatever reason they decided to keep him as a stallion and not geld him. Well, it doesn't matter what the reason but you now have a lot of responsibilities to handle with this stallion.

- Stallions are usually high strung at times and a lot to handle. They need to be carefully watched around other horses of either gender.
- The top priority with the stallion is discipline. You must take control of him and let him know you are the boss, not him.
- His nature is more aggressive and more fiery than a mare or a gelded miniature horse.
- The training program must be strict, whether it is pasture breeding or stall breeding.
- His genital areas must be washed before breeding is done. He must be handled daily. He needs to get use to these areas being touched so please do so during the daily grooming process.
- He needs a good nutritional meal program as well. He will be doing a lot of work so to speak.
- The main essential for him is a well-fitted nylon halter. This halter should only be used when you are handling your miniature horse stallion.
- Teach your stallion to understand the word "whoa." This command will be used a lot in his training and must be known by the horse.
- Training and lunging this stallion should be done in an area that is not a breeding area. You

don't want to confuse your miniature horse stallion.

- The horse should not confuse the halter and lead shank with breeding.
- The stallion's health is also a very important factor so keep an eye on that, as well. He must be disease free and be checked out for parasites too. He needs a good worming program also and daily exercise too.
- You can just turn him out in one of his pens and watch him kick, buck have fun out there. This is exercise for him too.
- His nutrition does increase his motility of his sperm and the number of them, so keep an eye on that.
- It's great for the owner to have respect and a mutual understanding with the stallion because they can and will be a handful at times, so be prepared.
- Determine early on what you will accept and will not accept from your stallion. Let him know his boundaries right from the start and stick with them. It's a good rule of thumb to follow and this way he knows what is expected of him and what you will not tolerate from him.
- A lot of horse owners do the pasture breeding with their stallions but I prefer the stall hand breeding. It's easier to do and to track.
- You have to make all these decisions for your stallion and stick to your plan once you do. You'll be happier you did and so will your stallion. Good luck with him!
- One must make changes in feeding after the breeding cycle is over. You must be constantly adjusting his nutritional needs from one season

to the next to accommodate his needs, at that time.

- The stallion is the most valuable asset in a breeding program. What he produces is important and will increase the value of your barn and foals if he produces better quality type miniature horses.
- The reason he is so important is he sires more than one foal a year while the broodmare can only produce one at a year if lucky.
- The year of breeding for a stallion can be divided up into four management and feeding periods. This would be post-breeding, non-breeding, pre-breeding and also breeding season.

The season for breeding ends for most breeders around July. Changes must be made at the end of season to change the stallion's attitude to that of non breeding time and adjust his feeding at this time.

The stallion should have two halters, one that is solely for breeding time and one that is for non-breeding time.

Everything must be changed to alter his attitude towards non-breeding time. He must graze more and exercise more frequently now. The stallion should become more relaxed within a few weeks after breeding season is over. Again you are in charge, not him and you must constantly remind him of this. Take control of your stallion, not the other way around. It's just the way it has to be to keep them under control. But they will be calmer in their down time when it's not breeding time for them. Exercise will take away some of that extra energy they have though. So, do that as much as possible for him to calm down. If the attitude of the horse remains in the breeding area then a forced exercise program is necessary.

Some miniature horse stallions do become thinner in the breeding season but this is not a concern, unless the horse is sick. Otherwise, just adjust his diet for the time being and see how that works for him.

Some stallions may develop teeth problems from the eating of their hay. A vet can take off these sharp points if it is necessary to do so. Stallions should also be on a deworming program from September to March in the year. It doesn't make any sense to deworm any miniature horse in the summer months either.

Stallions need a high energy feed with corn which allows them to thrive and not too much grain either. It all depends on the horse. You must make the decisions on what you think he needs, at the different times of the year. You don't need to add any supplements to their food either. As long as they have good hay, a quality pasture to graze in and a well balanced grain. More grain should be given during the breeding months and less the rest of the year. You must keep his nutrition in check.

During the pre-breeding season the key is to keep your miniature horse stallion in great shape. Keep him physically fit and also nutritionally ready for the breeding season to come. This is the most important time for the miniature horse stallion.

He must get a good quality grass, hay, alfalfa, or mixed hay during this time of year. This is a time when the horse is being prepared for four to four and a half months of the breeding season so it's a time to get him ready for this time in the year.

In mid-December place the horse on a regular schedule of exercise to prepare him for the months of breeding. His exercising is crucial to get him ready for the breeding months.

During the breeding season it's important to keep the stallion healthy and strong. He needs a great nutritional diet and some exercise but not as much.

You may want to now use a vitamin E supplement in his diet also. He should be fine with a well-balanced meal larger than the usual one though.

Stallions can be handled by older children, if you have trained them well. Stallions have to be kept in pens separated from all other mares and foals. Some geldings may be able to be in the same pens with them.

Stallions love to be outside, in any type of weather or time of year.

CHAPTER 7: EXERCISE, TRAINING AND HORSE SHOWING

EXERCISE

Exercise is a very important factor for you miniature horse. They should be exercised many times a week, even daily if possible.

Whether you are a seasoned veteran or a new miniature horse owner, chances are you will need a way to exercise your miniature horse daily. Your miniature horse can be lunged in a circle pen or any pen by holding a long lead out and having them run around you. Lunging is a great form or exercise for your horse and you to do. It provides what you need for a quick exercise routine. Lunging your horse will strengthen the horse's joints and muscles. It will also be a great way to build stamina and develop better balance for your horse too. It is also a good way to maintain fitness for a horse that does driving with a cart, and you don't even need to hook up the cart to do it. It also helps burn off some steam from a horse that's been stalled and it relieves some stress, as well.

To start lunging, you will first fit your horse properly with the right halter and lunge line. There are lunge lines made specifically to lunge all horse breeds and miniature horses also. Here is what you will need to get started with lunging your horse: A round pen or area to lunge in, a good fitting halter which is not too tight and fits properly, a lunge whip, a smooth lunge lead line-it should be cotton but could be nylon as well- and some gloves so you won't burn or hurt your hands lunging, if your horse should get spooked or pull away from you.

If this is your first time lunging your miniature horse, then you should do so in a closed area. That would be a good idea for you. A fence is a good idea to give your miniature horse some parameters and keep the horse somewhat more focused on what you intend to do with him or her. They'd be too distracted by an open area or field.

The part that most would find difficult with lunging your miniature horse would be to get the horse out on the circle to start with. If your horse tends to walk or trot with your leading than they shouldn't be too hard to get to lunge. Your body position should be opposite of the horse's shoulder, with your whip aimed behind the horse's rear end but not actually hitting the horse but rather the ground behind the horse.

To get started with lunging your miniature horse you will begin by facing the horse's hip. Right circle lunge line in your right hand and opposite when going left. This way you are in position to drive your miniature horse forward. When you first begin to lunge your horse may be full of itself but will soon calm down for you. You must communicate with your horse and make eye contact, teaching him or her to slow, stop and even reverse. It may sound difficult at first but will soon become second nature to you and your miniature horse with time and effort.

Young horses, especially yearlings, should not be lunged for more than about 15 to 20 minutes. Smaller circles can be too much on their joints. This is definitely enough time for them to get a good work out and relieve some stress. This will loosen their muscles and give them the exercise they need.

Remember to keep your circles larger and allow for warm-ups and also for cool off period afterwards. It's just like when humans choose to exercise. You must warm-up your muscles first and always have a cool down period after.

You can also lunge your show horse with many performance benefits to go along with it. You can use bridles with side reins that are attached and lunge that way too. This can also improve your horse's gait transitions by doing this method.

Cantering on the lunge line for the horse is not recommended. It's just too fast of a speed to control. So, you should not try to do this on the lunge line with your miniature horse. The slower gaits work better. A trot is probably the best gait to get the maximum results for your horse.

You may want to practice their jumping over jumps, if they are show horses. This too can be used as a form of exercise.

They do get some exercise by being in a field with other horses and playing around but this is probably not enough to keep their bodies in shape for showing or just in general.

Feeding and exercise should be well-balanced to keep your horse from getting overweight and under toned. Too little exercise will make this happen. Nothing is less pretty than an overweight miniature horse. It makes them look like a Dwarf or Midget horse and that they are not.

Exercise works all the horse's muscles and conditions them. It helps keep the horse healthy and active. It makes for a much happier miniature horse and they do not seem to mind this at all.

Pastured horses seldom exert themselves and don't get as much exercise as needed. You must make sure to maintain all the elements needed for the horse to be in shape. This includes feeding, properly grooming and also how much they exercise.

An hour of exercise daily is a good idea to start out with. Any form of exercise is a good thing for your miniature horse.

TRAINING OF YOUR MINIATURE HORSE

If you learn to control the miniature horse's mind, then his body will just naturally start to follow along. Many people have bought into the idea of that if they can control a horse's body they can also control their minds. It's actually the other way around with the horses. It takes development and trust on the horse's part with the owner.

To miniature horse show enthusiast, the training of the miniature horse for a show is a serious business.

The shows are very competitive and your horse must be in excellent shape with lots of training.

A halter is one of the most important equipment used on a horse. This is placed on its head in order to train or lead around. They are also not too expensive depending on the style you get. You'll need a leather one for showing and then one made of fabric is fine for around the barn.

There are many forms of training from liberty to pulling a cart to just plain lunging your horse. You have to decide what's best for you and your miniature horse.

You must start out slowly with your horse with exercise then work your way up, as your horse begins to increase in its stamina. You'll be able to see when your miniature horse has had enough, by the way they are acting or if they begin to become unruly or not listen to you. It's probably best to them stop until the next day. The miniature horse can only handle so much but as time goes by will be able to handle more and more.

Walking up and down inclines can be introduced once your horse develops more muscle tone. You should just begin with lead lunging first until that happens.

HORSE SHOWS

There is nothing more beautiful than a miniature horse groomed from head to toe for a show. They look much different clipped down for the show ring than in the winter time with their winter coats on.

The miniature horse needs to be on a strict nutritional diet before going to show to get into optimum shape for this event.

They must be exercised regularly and have regular farrier visits, as well.

Grooming for the show is a year round thing that must be done regularly especially if you're going to show your horse. It's important to take pride in doing this for your horse to look good at the time of the shows.

After the winter time the horses must be clipped. Either what is called a "full body clip" of a "show shave." Whatever you choose to call it must be done in order to show your miniature horse at its best. It makes a world of difference to the appearance of your miniature horse and how it looks.

Most minis are clipped for shows and the judges will show a preference to those that are groomed nicely and clipped. I personally haven't seen any at a show that were not fully groomed and clipped.

The shaved horse will lose much of its color on its coat, but the horse will look better and more defined by clipping it. It will just appear lighter or darker depending on its color to begin with. This is most important in halter classes.

If you are showing in the obstacles or driving classes only a sleeker appearance will be acceptable to the judges. The classes in performance have less emphasis on grooming perfection of your miniature horse. There are no rules on body clipping; it's totally up to the owner or person showing the horse. But it is good to put your horse's best hoof forward and have him or her well groomed no matter what.

You can dye your horse's mane or tail if they are getting bleached out by the sun. There are no rules regarding this either. I like to stay natural with things but some do decide to take this route with their miniature horses.

Please blanket your horse if it's been clipped and you want to keep the horse clean or in some cases warmer. The blanket will keep some of the dust off your horse after bathing and clipping the horse.

Once you have blankets for your horse, decide the best time to clip it and use them to keep the horse warm or cleaner.

Miniature horses are almost always clipped before all shows they go to. This is the rule of thumb for clipping for the shows. You don't want you r horse to start lacking in the grooming department.

You have to decide the best time to clip the horse. Some white horses are done right before the show to avoid looking pink. But usually you can get away with a day or two before the show.

The blade size on your clippers will affect the length and color of your horse. Generally you just clip all the way down but if your horse has a nicer color a little longer you can adjust the blades to suit your style or your horses' style.

Remember the larger the blade size the closer the clip of the horse is. The majority of the mini horses are clipped with 10 blades; some go a bit smaller for color reasons. It's totally up to what you like on your horses. You can try out a cheaper clipper which might work well for you but it's trial and error with what kind you want to use or what's best for you. But some cheaper ones work just as well as the more expensive ones. Just maintain whatever clippers you can afford and that should work out for you. It depends on what your budget is for you. Clipping is an important part of showing. SO, go for more advanced clippers if you are showing; if not you can go for more affordable ones if you are not showing. That's how I'd do it.

Keep your clippers clean and working. Brand new blades must be soaked before using them and also you will need oil to oil them up while using them, as well.

Remember to bathe your horse before starting to clip them. Give the horse a good cleaning and then when ready you can take on the art of clipping your horse. You'll be so happy once you finish and see how your horse turns out for you. They look just beautiful after they are clipped. So, remember to never clip a dirty horse. It's much easier if they are free of dust and dirt.

You can start to clip as soon as the head, neck and back are dry on the horse. It's best to clip them right after they are dry as soon as you can after their bath is done. It's the best time to clip the horse while it's free from the dust and dirt that they gather in their coats, manes and tails.

Don't forget to have your show sheen handy for after their bath and clipping. This will make their coat look absolutely wonderful and in tip top shape for you. Also, some fly spray is also good to keep on hand to help out your horse, as well.

Horse shows for miniature horses are done all throughout the world and all over the United States.

Your horse must be registered with AMHA, to be shown.

There are many classes in these shows, such as halter, supreme halter, jumping, dressage, liberty and also many cart classes, as well.

In order to get ready for a show your miniature horse should be in shape and well trained. Also, they need to look their best and be clipped down and presentable to show them. Their hooves should be polished black also.

If you are interested in getting into the show arena, my suggestion is you seek help from professionals in getting your horse ready for the ring. They are fun for children to participate in also and they have many age oriented classes for them to show in, as well. It's a very competitive thing for many of the miniature horse show enthusiasts but with training and preparation you'll be a pro in no time.

Lunging is a very good way to exercise your horse. It can also be used as a warm-up exercise for other activities.

When you lunge a miniature horse every once in a while you should change the direction of the horse.

A miniature horse must be set up correctly in order to jump the jump right. Their hooves need to be placed in the correct position of the horse.

The pole on the ground before the jump lets the horse know when to start its jump over the jumps.

When jumping a horse over a jump or obstacle you must pretend that you are jumping over the jump, as well.

A miniature horse can be trained to pull a person around. This is fine for older children but younger children should ride with an adult.

Treats can be used for training purposes, when leading a horse around or getting them in the conformation position required for performing in horse shows.

Only certain miniature horses are able to pull carts, due to the weight of the cart and the person on it. It is usually wise to use a bigger mini weighing a larger amount for this.

Most horses enjoy training in any type of weather to stay in shape and healthy.

This is the set up of the cart with the reins attached to it. Some help may be required when starting out, until you get a hang of it.

Driving a horse takes some time to learn but with practice you'd be able to do it soon enough.

Most horses actually like to drive a cart and don't mind doing it. They can go up to a canter safely with this cart but usually would go just at a trot.

85

Showing a horse is great fun for anyone, especially for children of all ages.

You can win many ribbons at any age, at shows around the country.

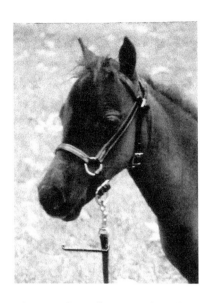

This is what a show horse's head looks like.

This is a way of training a show horse before a show. Anyone of any age can train their own miniature horses.

Showing a horse or a miniature horse has many rewards for not only adults but for children. It gives them great self esteem and something to do that makes them very happy.

Showing has many rewards but winning the national championship is the ultimate prize for a miniature horse owner and/or trainer.

These are what show horse look like in the show ring. They are clipped down for showing with their show leather halters and leads.

CHAPTER 8: TRAILERS AND TRANSPORTING MINIATURE HORSES

TRAILERS

There are many types of trailers, some with living areas in them and some without. Some that are larger that can also accommodate full-sized horses. You can also get smaller, sized-down ones for miniature horses.

You may or may not need a trailer but mostly you will. If ever an emergency arises where a horse must be transported to an animal hospital, you would want to have one or access to one of these trailers.

There are many things to decide in buying a trailer, just as in buying a miniature horse. You must figure out what type you want and how much you can afford to spend on it. You must figure out if you need to have living courters in it or not, and if you want a larger one with its versatilities or just a smaller one for transporting the miniature horses without the living area for you to use to sleep.

You will need a trailer if you choose to show your miniature horses. You might want to consider one with the living area for you and your family to sleep in, instead of booking a hotel or motel to stay in. Either way there is a lot to think over with this big decision you have.

TRANSPORTING YOUR MINIATURE HORSE

You must minimize shipping stress while transporting you r miniature horses. It can be a stressful time for your miniature horse and making it as comfortable as possible is a good idea but at the same time making it a safe trip is important as well.

This is an unnatural time for them and this causes much of the stress. They get stressed due to the vehicle's vibrations plus the confinement of the area you place them in, in the trailer. Also, they try to balance themselves and this causes stress too. As time goes by they may get more use to it, if they have to do it a lot for showing.

One of the biggest problems with transporting them is the fumes and poor ventilations. Then we compound the problem with tying up our horse's heads, so they can't move much. This causes them not to be able to lower their heads to naturally drain out their respiratory ducts of dust, mucus and other things clogging them. So, they are breathing in stale air and dust from the hay in there.

The dust getting in their lungs is usually the cause for shipping fever they may get at times.

Their immune system can go down if shipped for long distances so keep a close eye on them and minimize any stress that you can.

If the trip is more than 12 hours, try to stop at that time and continue the next day or at least take a couple hours of rest at some point for the horses.

Make sure to ensure some airflow for the miniature horses with the trailer. That will help out a lot with this situation.

After a long trip when you get back from it, give your horses a few days to recover. Don't exercise or over work them. Just let them relax a few days and get back into the groove of things. It's important after a long trip to do this for the horse and let them just recuperate for a few days or even a week. The trip is not a natural thing for them to do, so they really do need this time.

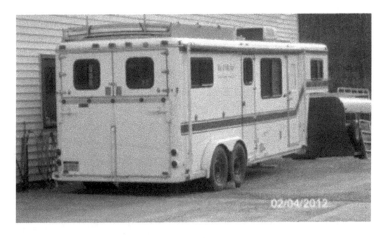

This is a big horse trailer made for miniature horses, with a living area in it. This can haul about 6 miniatures, depending on their sizes.

These trailers can be customized for miniature horses to ride in. They make them for full-sized horses too but without the living area in them.

This is a smaller sized down trailer made for miniature horses. It can comfortably fit at least four miniature horses in it.

CHAPTER 9: WHERE CAN I BUY A MINIATURE HORSE?

WHERE TO BUY MINIATURE HORSES

Buying a horse is easy, but buying the right one takes some time and effort on your part. You need to investigate the situation and even have your vet do an initial purchase exam if you want to have that done also. It's important with the cost of the miniature horse, that you do make the right decision. You have to first decide on a mare, stallion or gelded miniature horse and then from what farm you will be buying one for. You can look around and don't rush yourself on this important decision.

Miniature horses are very common nowadays and they are not necessarily all expensive. You can get pet quality miniature horses for a fraction of the cost, if you decide it's a pet and not a show horse. That's totally up to you and what you want to do with your miniature horse.

There are many breeders around the world and throughout the United States. You can look them up on the internet and find the right one for you.

There are also many miniature horse magazines which many farms advertise their horses for sale in. This is also a great method to use also.

Every year thousands of pet-quality miniature horses are sent to slaughter and The Guide Horse

Foundation recommends that you consider adopting an unwanted, abused or recued miniature horse from a horse rescue organization. Or you could buy from an auction, as well.

There are lots of online miniature horse sales and owner posted miniature horses for sale on the web. There are many ways to go about this these days.

There are many auction houses or auction sales where you can also get a good deal on a miniature horse or miniature horses for your farm. They have great sales on the miniature horse breed and you can get a great deal there. You can look these auctions up online or check them out in Miniature Horse World magazine. That should give you an idea of where these auctions are being held and when they are being held. You might just get a good enough deal on you r mini horse and decide to get a friend to take home with him or her. It's a great idea to have at least two, so they do have another horse to socialize and entertain themselves with. Once you get one, you usually always want more anyway.

Also, for those who need them there are guide horses available. Guide horses regularly work indoors leading their handler to shopping malls, offices and restaurants. When they are off-duty they prefer to stay outdoors in their barn and stall. All miniature horses to be used as guide horses, are required to pass a physical exam prior to being selected for this great service. They must have good health and sound legs plus demonstrate stamina. They must also be less than 26 inches high at the withers. They are constantly watched for health concerns by a licensed vet. They are great asset to their blind owner and can be of great help to them but also great companionship, as well.

You can buy miniature horses at many farms, around the country. They are located throughout the web online or in miniature horse magazines.

Miniature horses are the most unique gift to give yourself and can be located in lots of different places. The internet is the best route to take or just plain word of mouth. Either way I hope you find the mini of your dreams!

CHAPTER 10: OTHER INFORMATION

QUICK FACTS

Miniature horses are considered "horses" and part of the horse breed. Many try to refer to them as ponies but that is the incorrect term for these great little horses. It is considered an insult to many miniature horses owners and breeders when these horses are referred to as "ponies." They were made into a separate horse breed by the AMHA many years ago.

There are 240,000 miniature horses worldwide.

The miniature horse can sleep in many different positions. They can sleep in the upright position, and also in a lying down position, mainly while young but also when older too. They usually are pretty observant and don't sleep for very long. Usually many times throughout the day and night, you'll find them sleeping. They are very light sleepers, as well.

The wear and tear on horse's teeth does tell their age. A good veterinarian will be able to tell how old a horse or your horse is by looking at the wear on their teeth. The miniature horse's teeth do change in color, becoming yellow or with brown over many years. This is just a natural process with the aging of the miniature horse.

Miniature horses need a salt block to lick and can drink many gallons of water per day. They need a lot of water to survive, as do humans and other types of animals. Please make sure they have clean drinking water to drink throughout the day. If they are in a pasture, then leaving them a bucket to drink from out there is a very good idea, as well.

You can get your miniature horse shoed by a farrier but it's not necessary. However, doing so would keep their hooves in better shape. The farrier usually trims down the hoof before putting the horseshoes on. The horseshoe is then shaped while it's hot from the fire.

Miniature horses can do obstacles such as jumps and different types of obstacles that you set up. You'd be surprised at how they can actually jump. The owner or trainer must lead the miniature horse up to the jump, as they jump over it. Usually the owner or trainer would first warm-up the horse possibly through lunging or some sort of type of exercise, to get them ready for jumping. The horse uses many gaits to jump over these jumps. They start out in a walk and end up in a cantor or even a gallop, after jumping over the jump.

Saddles are available for these horses but only children under 5 years old or under 50 pounds can use them. It's a great fun activity for them but use a bigger miniature horse for the riding, one that would be able to handle the small child's weight. They can be ridden either English or Western, as well.

There are classes in shows for these miniature horses wear they wear costumes along with their owner or trainer in the show arena.

The domestic donkey, Poitou donkey and African donkey are cousins of the horse breed. Also, the tapir and the rhinoceros are distant cousins of the horse breed, as well. It's interesting to know who is related to the horse. Who would have thought the Rhino was related to the miniature horse or horse breed?

The parts of the miniature horse are as follows: the cheek, the throttle, the shoulder, the breast, the forearm, the knees, the cannon, the pastern, the coronet, the fetlock, the elbow, the hook, the foot, the point of the hock, the point of the rump, the root of the tail or dock, the croup, the hip, the flank, the withers and the crest.

You measure your miniature horse at the withers, which is at the end of the mane and go all the way down from there to the ground measuring by inches. The miniature horse should be under 34 inches in length from that point to be considered a true miniature horse, in the miniature horse breed.

Miniature horses are very friendly, ponies are more timid and tend to run away from people more. The nature of the miniature horse is much more people friendly and this is what makes them so great for children, as well as adults. They will love you back in great ways and they are so easy going in their mannerisms.

They can also drive cars well too. They make smaller sized down carts that you can buy for these unique smaller miniature horses. They are very beautiful and a fun way for your family to enjoy their miniature horses also.

Miniature horses can cost anywhere from pet quality of as little as $1000.00 and go up to over $200,000 for a horse with great bloodlines. Some you can't even put a value on them because the owner would not sell them to anyone.

There is also a color of minis that is a cross between an appaloosa and a pinto, called a "Pintaloosa."

Miniature horses are measured in inches instead of hands like the full-sized breed of horse is measured.

Miniature horses can usually be ridden by children up to the age of 5 years old or up to about 50 pounds of weight.

Miniature horses can be kept with bigger horses. They just need a smaller sized down stall for them to look out of. So, you would just need different sized stalls to keep both of them. They do interact well together outside but usually would be put in separate pens but it would not be impossible to put them together, as well.

Be careful with the bit you use for driving. It should not affect your miniature horse's teeth. The bit in the horse's mouth should never contact the cheek of your horse.

Discoloration in your horse's teeth shows that something may be wrong with your horse's health. You can tell a lot by checking your horse's teeth regularly. They do show health issues and other things, as well.

Your vet may check your horse's teeth for signs of trouble now and again. It's a good rule of thumb to keep an eye on them.

Forty thousand chews per day by your miniature horses can cause substantial tooth abrasion. Teeth do erupt and move out of their bone during the horse's lifetime also. Some do begin to lose their teeth over time and 20% of their teeth do become over worn over time also.

Horses have a high capacity for remembering the emotional feelings surrounding a particular set of circumstances created.

If you learn to control a miniature horse's mind, then his body will just naturally follow along with it.

Having good ground work for your horse is about using the horse's mind through an good emotional experience. This will help guide the horse with most anything, if you use this theory with them.

You can use groundwork to gain your horse's confidence with you.

If a miniature horse makes a mistake, you don't give up on him or say he is unmanageable. You just need to change how you deal with the situation better next time.

Each horse is different in how you approach things with them. Once you get to know your horse, you will be able to know what's needed to train them and communicate with them. They all react to situations differently.

Trial and error is a good way to go when starting to train your miniature horse. Just see what works best with him or her and then go from there. You just need to try different things because each horse will react differently to different situations and approaches on things. Just try your best to get to know your horse and his or her reaction to everything. It's the best way to go when starting out with your new miniature horse.

The reality of miniature horse training is that it is a mental game played in a physical medium. But you must let the horse know who's in charge, at all times or they will take advantage of your good nature at times.

One of the biggest mistakes people can make with their relationships with their miniature horses is not paying attention to things going on with the horse. Not just physically or nutritionally but also mentally. It's important to know your miniature horse well and then you will both succeed because of it.

Horses have the ability to find their way home by using the scents of their markings. This is not unusual for them. They have a great ability as do a lot of animals to use their scents or smells for many things.

Horses know a lot about one another by smelling each other. Scents tell them a lot of information.

Working with stallions will probably be your most difficult battle but if properly trained they will listen to your voice and command. But you must be stern and always in charge of them. They can be a handful but are well worth your time and effort, in the end of all of the training and everything else.

A horse utilizes both eyes and the horse's retina is adapted for the detection of movement. He uses both eyes until something approaches within three to four feet of him or her, then it is forced to lower its head and use one eye to focus on it.

Always remember that miniature horses do have the differing personalities, just as full-sized horses and all other horse breeds. They do have their moods too but are naturally sweet in nature. They are good for kids because of their size and lovingness they have about them. But you must remember that they are still horses.

Never stand directly behind a miniature horse or any horse breed. Just because of their size doesn't mean they can't get spooked and kick. If you know your horse well enough that they do not kick then that would be a different story but always be aware of their behaviors or if they seem to be acting differently on that day. You just must be careful around them at times. Don't let their size fool you.

Some believe in the miniature horse world that men handle stallions more effectively than women due to their strength but I do think that either gender could handle them well if properly trained. It's really not about strength, but playing a mental game with them not a physical game. As a trainer you are not a man or a woman but rather a presence to the horse. If you do the training right the horse will prevail regardless of what sex you are. You must just understand your horse's actions and know how to handle them correctly. You can just make friends with your horse and let him know that you are in charge. That should help the situation a lot of the time.

Due to advancements in health, nutrition and the management of horses, the breed is living longer than ever. If you keep up with your horse, he or she may live well over 20 years old. It's a lifetime commitment from you, as they do live a long time. Some can live up to 35 years or more. We have a few horses close to 25 years old at this time in our two barns. So, it is very possible for them to live a long, healthy and happy life with you by their side. So, don't take the buying of them without serious consideration. It's not to be taken lightly; it's a big step in one's life.

Most miniature horses and all horse breeds would constantly eat and overeat if they could. This is not healthy and this is especially true for the smaller horse breeds and miniature horses. They would get so overweight and not look so wonderful. A little too much weight on them is not good and does not look good. It makes them look short and stumpy. Please keep a close eye on what you feed your miniature horse and of course how much you feed them. It's important to the health and nutrition of your miniature horse. Over feeding them is a definite no-no and you will have to be very careful also if deciding to show your horse. Exercise and nutrition would be the most important things to watch out for plus the horse's health too.

When horses are bored they tend to overeat. Some people do place some safe toys in their stalls for them to have some activities. You could place a ball above their head to play with from a string but safely put it in their stalls. Foals enjoy kicking the ball around their stalls too. There are many things you can do to relieve some of their boredom but over feeding them is not one of the things you should do at all.

There are specialized nets available to feed your horses hay they are hung from the gates or within their stalls. When they are ready to eat they can just pull it through the net to eat. This does seem to entertain them a bit and gives them more to do. This slows down their eating a little too. So, they don't get as much at once.

Beet pulp added to your horse's food is a great way to bulk up their meals. It's another type of feed for your horses. This feed won't add too many calories to your horse's diet either. If your horse won't eat beet pulp, most do but if they won't just add a handful of their sweet grain to it and they will gobble it up I'm sure.

Just an interesting fact here that flies are more attracted to darker colored horses like brown or black ones and less attracted to the white ones. So, be sure to use more fly spray on your darker horses to prevent them from the annoyance of them bothering them.

Paris Hilton now owns a beautiful miniature horse. Also, some of our miniature horse friends sold some minis to Aerosmith's lead singer, Steven Tyler and band members too.

We have been on many news programs many years ago and even Good Morning America and the Regis & Kathy Lee show with our miniature horses. But that was a very long time ago and when the miniature horses were first becoming popular and known around the United States of America.

Showing miniature horses is very rewarding and fun for all age groups. They have many classes for all and prizes plus ribbons for your efforts in the show. They have shows around this country and in other countries, as well. Some states here in the United States have them year round, as the weather is permitting for them. Here in the north they are more in the springtime and summertime months.

There is even a national show at the end of the show season in October which is usually held down south or even in Nevada some years. They have had this show in Florida, Louisiana, Oklahoma, Texas and New Mexico. It's given to the warmer states to host each year, as it's in the wintertime. It's a great opportunity if you make the cut to advance to this show. It's nice to see all the horses from around the country participating. It's all the best of the best in the country that are there to be shown and seen by all. If you just want to go as a spectator or even to show your miniature horse also, than this is the show to make it to. Plus, you could or would gain valuable knowledge there. All the best handlers are there with their show ready championship miniature horses.

You can find all your shows and show dates listed in the Miniature Horse World magazine or look up AMHA on the internet for all that type of information on your miniature horses. But I would definitely subscribe to the Miniature Horse World magazine, as soon as possible for all your horse needs type information. It is a great source for any information including health concerns and just regular farm information or horse sales. But it is the most informative magazine out there on your miniature horse or if you are planning on buying one. We have also been seen in this miniature horse magazine. Our farm has been featured with our miniature horses. It's actually a really beautiful magazine to look at; the horse pictures are just incredible in it.

Elderly horses or senior horses may need some extra care from you and their vet but they can stay healthy through a good nutritional and exercise program. They may get arthritis and other ailments so just keep an extra eye on taking good care of them. After all, they do bring you joy!

There do come some sad times, when we must take a horse out of the agony they are in from either old age or a disease that is consuming them. It may be a terminal illness that has taken a great toll on them or whatever the case may be. Or even a terrible accident they've had. In this case, it's best to quietly have them euthanized.   Unfortunately times like this come about but we must do what's best for the horse. They must not suffer in pain, at all. You'll have to weigh the decision, as to if this is the right time to do this. You will know by the condition of your horse, if it is indeed the right time for you and the miniature horse. They can't be replaced but you have the cherished memories close to your heart.

Miniature horses are one of the most unique, precious gifts you can have. They are great for children and adults alike. You can have them as pets or show them around the country. They are enjoyable to all and have great personalities. You don't have to spend a lot of money for a pet quality one to love and care for. You may just get one but you usually end up with a lot more to care for. No one can buy just one and be happy with just having one. So, be prepared to share your love and receive back in full from these wonderful creatures that God has brought us.

Miniature horses are a great way to entertain and delight your family, friends and children of all ages. They are a great way to show your love and receive it back from them, as well. They cost less to keep then bigger horses because they eat less and take up less room too.

Raising miniature horses is a great experience but one that does take effort and time. It takes kind, compassionate people with a love for the horse breed. It is rewarding to all those involved and can be like no other experience you may have. So, hopefully you'll decide to try raising, training, showing or just loving miniature horses too!

There are many books and information out there on the internet and in specialized magazines for miniature horses. You can find all that you're looking for and more out there. I recommend the magazine called Miniature Horse World for anyone interested in getting into miniature horses. It has a lot of useful information to get you started out in the field of miniature horses.

About the Expert

Christina Reilly was born in Suffern, New York in 1969. She grew-up in Westchester County in New York, then moved to Orange County, New York and has lived there for the past 30 years. She has a loving family with her mother, father, two sisters, two daughters and a son. She is now living with her loving fiancé, at this time in southeastern New York. The expert has helped to raise miniature horses most of her life, since the age of 13 years old. Her family has two farms. One is located in Orange County, New York and one is located in upstate New York. The family has enjoyed raising miniature horses for a long time now and hopes to inspire others to do the same!

HowExpert publishes quick 'how to' guides on all topics from A to Z by everyday experts. Visit HowExpert.com to learn more.

Recommended Resources

- HowExpert.com – Quick 'How To' Guides on All Topics from A to Z by Everyday Experts.
- HowExpert.com/free – Free HowExpert Email Newsletter.
- HowExpert.com/books – HowExpert Books
- HowExpert.com/courses – HowExpert Courses
- HowExpert.com/clothing – HowExpert Clothing
- HowExpert.com/membership – HowExpert Membership Site
- HowExpert.com/affiliates – HowExpert Affiliate Program
- HowExpert.com/writers – Write About Your #1 Passion/Knowledge/Expertise & Become a HowExpert Author.
- HowExpert.com/resources – Additional HowExpert Recommended Resources
- YouTube.com/HowExpert – Subscribe to HowExpert YouTube.
- Instagram.com/HowExpert – Follow HowExpert on Instagram.
- Facebook.com/HowExpert – Follow HowExpert on Facebook.